Teeny-Tiny
TURNTABLE

T0344116

Printed in China

15 14 13 12 11
Digit on the right indicates the number of this printing

ISBN 978-0-7624-6235-3

Published by Running Press Book Publishers,
An Imprint of Perseus Books, LLC,
A Subsidiary of Hachette Book Group, Inc.

1290 Avenue of the Americas,
New York, NY 10104
Visit us on the web!
www.runningpress.com

DO NOT MIX OLD AND NEW BATTERIES

BACK
to
VINYL

AS DIGITAL DOWNLOAD SALES HAVE
taken a fall over the past few years, one
music wave that has enjoyed a revival
is vinyl, which now accounts for more
than $346.8M in worldwide sales.

Imagine a time when, if there was
a song or album you wanted to own,
you had to actually go out to a record
store, rather than just download it
with the click of a button. For music

lovers, this time was also about record collecting, which became a passionate hobby for many, especially those on the hunt for rare records, as well as albums from revered artists.

So why—all of a sudden—the renewed interest in LPs? Maybe it's the collectability factor, the artwork, or the crisp, satisfying grooves on that round wax disc—whatever it is, you know you can expect a close, personal connection to your favorite song or artist—along with a string of comforting pops, crackles, and hisses.

Using Your
TEENY-TINY
TURNTABLE

YOUR *TEENY-TINY TURNTABLE* KIT
consists of a mini record player and
three mini records; each record
plays one song. Simply raise the
hinged lid, place a record down on
the platter, spin, and the music will
play. When you're ready to hear a
new song, switch out the record for
a new one.

OUR 10 FAVORITE
Chart-Topping
RECORD ALBUMS

IT WAS QUITE THE TASK NARROWING down our favorite vinyl LPs, but here is a list of ten of our favorites, listed in order of release date.

1

THE JIMI HENDRIX EXPERIENCE

ARE YOU EXPERIENCED

(RELEASED IN AUGUST, 1967, IN THE U.S.)

REGARDED AS ONE OF THE GREATEST records in the history of rock music, *Are You Experienced* was recorded over the course of five months in London, and it ranked at No. 5 on the *Billboard* 200 in the U.S. This record stood out for tracks that represented several genres of music, including R&B, blues, and rock, with favorites including "Foxy Lady," "Hey Joe," and "Purple Haze." The cover art for the U.S. edition featured a psychedelic-looking Jimi Hendrix Experience accompanied by bumpy, far-out lettering and a bright yellow background.

2

THE BEATLES
ABBEY ROAD
(RELEASED IN SEPTEMBER, 1969)

ONE OF THE BEST-SELLING BEATLES albums of all time, *Abbey Road* was one of the last albums that the band recorded all together in recording sessions. Some of the album's best known songs include "Come Together," "Octopus' Garden," and "Here Comes the Sun." The cover art features the Beatles crossing London's Abbey Road at a crosswalk outside of Abbey Road Studios. It has become one of the most famous album covers of all time, as well as one of the most likely album covers to be imitated. Thousands of Beatles fans visit the famous zebra crossing every year to take a stroll across the road like their favorite band.

Fun Fact

Records are typically twelve inches and have an A side and a B side, each of which makes up one half of the album. They are packaged in clear plastic or cardboard sleeves for protection. On the inside, the records are packaged in paper liners, to keep out dust; these liners include circular cut-outs so the name of the album is still visible. The cardboard sleeve is also sometimes a gatefold that includes special inserts like lyric sheets, perforated postcards, and posters.

THE
ROLLING STONES
EXILE ON MAIN ST.
(RELEASED IN MAY, 1972)

ALTHOUGH IT ORIGINALLY RECEIVED less than stellar reviews from critics, *Exile on Main St.* was later lauded as one of the best albums of all time, and reached No. 1 worldwide. By this time, Keith Richards was hooked on heroin and the band members showed different levels of commitment to each other, so tracks were recorded slowly, eventually resulting in "Happy," "I Just Want to See His Face," and "All Down the Line." The cover ended up featuring images of circus freaks and performers from documentary photographer Robert Frank's collection; the photos of the band, taken by Norman Seeff, that were originally planned for the cover ended up as postcards inside the album sleeve.

4

PINK FLOYD
THE DARK SIDE
OF THE MOON
(ORIGINALLY RELEASED IN MARCH, 1973)

PINK FLOYD WAS KNOWN FOR ITS USE
of musique concrète and synthesizers;
each side of this album had a cont-
inuous piece of music, without any
breaks between tracks. The music

on the album is meant to reflect themes of human life and the human experience, including money, greed, unity, time, death, and mental illness, with tracks such as "Breathe," "Time," "Money," and "Eclipse." In response to keyboardist Richard Wright's request for "simple and bold," the cover art's iconic image is a prism with a rainbow.

Fun Fact

The cover of the record album is considered by some to be just as important as the record itself, and many have even gone on to win Grammys for their album artwork. Many notable artists have designed and art directed album covers including Andy Warhol (The Rolling Stones, The Velvet Underground), Hipgnosis (Pink Floyd, Led Zeppelin), Rex Ray (David Bowie), and Shepard Fairey (Johnny Cash), to name just a few.

5

ELTON JOHN
GOODBYE YELLOW BRICK ROAD

(RELEASED IN OCTOBER, 1973)

RELEASED AT THE PEAK OF ELTON JOHN'S popularity, this album was originally set to record in Jamaica, but recording sessions were moved to France after the band experienced issues with the sound studio and piano, as well as violent political tensions. The move to the Château d'Hérouville gave John so much inspiration for material that he ended up recording a double album with a total of seventeen songs, including hits like "Candle in the Wind," "Bennie and the Jets," and the album's title song. The album was inducted into the Grammy Hall of Fame in 2003 and has sold more than 30M copies worldwide.

BRUCE SPRINGSTEEN
BORN TO RUN
(RELEASED IN AUGUST, 1975)

AFTER A SHAKY START WITH HIS FIRST
two albums, Bruce Springsteen made
a comeback with the release of
Born to Run, which hit No. 3 on the
Billboard 200 and sold more than
6M copies in the U.S. It is considered
one of the greatest albums of all
time, with hits like "Thunder Road,"

"Tenth Avenue Freeze-Out," and the album's title song. The image on the cover was taken by Eric Meola and shows Springsteen holding an electric guitar and leaning against saxophonist Clarence Clemons. The iconic pose has been imitated frequently, and Springsteen and Clemons even repeated the pose during concerts in dim lighting, much to the amusement of their fans, only to quickly pull away and break the pose before the lights came back.

Fun Fact

The back of the record usually included notes about the album from music critics, which continued running on the album's inner protective liner, hence the name *liner notes*. The notes usually included lyrics and commentary about the tracks, as well as credits for the album and the name of the record label. The notes were also often a place for critics to not only comment on what they thought about the tracks in general, but also to discuss the political or social significance of the lyrics at a time of social discontent.

QUEEN
A NIGHT AT THE OPERA
(RELEASED IN NOVEMBER, 1975)

THE TITLE FOR THIS ALBUM WAS LIFTED from the Marx Brothers' film *A Night at the Opera*, which the band members watched one night while recording the album in their studio. The record became the band's first platinum-selling record in the U.S., hitting No. 4 on the *Billboard* 200 and going on to sell over 6M copies. Notable tracks from the album include "You're My Best Friend," "I'm In Love with My Car," and "Bohemian Rhapsody," the latter going on to win two Grammy Award nominations, and to become arguably the most popular rock song in history.

DAVID BOWIE
LET'S DANCE
(RELEASED IN APRIL, 1983)

LET'S DANCE **IS DAVID BOWIE'S BEST-**
selling album, with more than 10.7M
copies sold worldwide. The blues-rock
album produced hits like "China Girl,"
"Modern Love," and "Let's Dance,"
the latter of which became Bowie's
only No. 1 hit in both the U.S. and the
U.K. The popularity and variety of the

album brought in a larger mainstream audience, but made Bowie feel as if he had to cater to them for his next two albums, which consequently were not able to meet the same level of success. Bowie ended up forming a hard rock band shortly after, called Tin Machine, in order to re-launch himself artistically.

Fun Fact

In 1958 the Recording Industry Association of America (RIAA) established a program to keep track of record album sales and help determine which albums became best-sellers. Originally an album would get a Gold Award for $1M in sales. In 1975 the system changed from sales dollars to the number of copies sold. If a record sells 500,000 copies, it is awarded Gold. If it sells 1M copies, it is awarded Platinum. If it sells 2M copies it is awarded Multi-platinum, and if it sells 10M copies it receives the Diamond Award.

BOB MARLEY
AND THE WAILERS
LEGEND
(RELEASED IN MAY, 1984)

***LEGEND* IS A COLLECTION OF BOB** Marley's most well-known hit singles and is considered the greatest and best-selling reggae album of all time. Originally released three years after Marley's death, the tracks included powerful political messages and

Jamaican soul from the world's favorite Rastafarian, with stand-outs like "No Woman, No Cry," "I Shot the Sheriff," and "Redemption Song." The album spent the fourth longest run in history on the *Billboard* 200, at 413 weeks, has sold about 25M copies globally, and is the second longest-charting album in the history of *Billboard* magazine.

MADONNA
LIKE A VIRGIN
(RELEASED IN NOVEMBER, 1984)

LIKE A VIRGIN WAS MADONNA'S FIRST
album to hit No. 1 on the *Billboard*
200 and sold more than 21M records
worldwide, making it one of the best-
selling albums of all time. Both the
songs "Like a Virgin" and "Material
Girl" were defining songs for Madonna
and became No. 1 and No. 2 hits,

respectively, on the *Billboard* 100. In 1985, Madonna became the first female artist to sell 5M copies in the U.S. and was declared the top pop artist of the year. The image of Madonna in a provocative white wedding dress on the cover plays with the idea of Madonna as the Roman Catholic name for the Virgin Mary, as well as the concept of the virgin birth.

Fun Fact

One of the oldest record stores in the world is Spillers Records in Cardiff, Wales, which was founded in 1894 by Henry Spiller. Spillers survived, but in the early '90s other record stores were forced to either shut their doors or adopt carrying CDs instead. When digital downloads became the norm and even CDs lost their popularity, more shops were forced to close down. As the resurgence of vinyl has taken off again, however, many new record shops are popping up and old record shops are enjoying the spike in profits.

THIS BOOK HAS BEEN BOUND USING
HANDCRAFT METHODS AND SMYTH–
SEWN TO ENSURE DURABILITY.

THE COVER AND INTERIOR WERE
DESIGNED BY AMANDA RICHMOND.

THE TEXT WAS WRITTEN BY
JORDANA TUSMAN.

THE TEXT WAS EDITED BY
SHANNON LEE CONNORS.

THE TEXT WAS SET IN
HANLEY AND BRANDON.